PRAISE FOR BERGMAN'S ISLAND AND OTHER POEMS

"Award-winning author Kate Christensen once said that 'Nostalgia is a powerful drug.' In times of personal duress, we may find ourselves engaging in what psychologists call 'euphoric recall.' It is an overly idealized reconstruction of the past. One of the strongest themes in Ralph Monday's *Bergman's Island and Other Poems* is that of nostalgia. The speakers range from the walking, war-torn dead longing for life in 'Lost German Girl' to the broken and lonely searching for human connections in 'Dirty Moons' and even includes a manifestation of Wallace Stevens' languid heroine who now sees 'Sunday Morning' from more worldly, cynical eyes. This nostalgia is a painkiller, a meticulously crafted psychological narcotic distilled from a foggy past into a simpler, more naive time of drugstore counters and quiet dusty roads populated by Rockwell smiles and the rounded fenders of postwar Packards; an inoculation to combat the present. Monday has offered us not a fix to keep us glassy-eyed while we numb ourselves, but instead a *cure* for our disease, 'A Prayer for Those That are Plugged In.' In this, we also find another pervasive theme of Monday's collection: the very real tragic nature of nostalgia. It drips and pools in such pieces as 'Waiting' and 'What Good is Love?' and seems to scream 'Why can't we go back? Why must it always be forward' in 'Still Life with Random Thoughts.' Monday tells us the hard-won wisdom of a simpler past may be the cure for our existential woes, but like a massive monument that looms on the horizon, it appears much closer than it really is. As Monday reminds us in 'Same Old Song,' 'We all want to return from exile, somehow, someway, but Wolfe was right, no way home again.'" — Matt Hundley

"Ralph Monday's *Bergman's Island and Other Poems* is an homage to Western civilization and mythology. History books tell the facts of history, but art, particularly poetry, describes events and culture through the experience of the people. Monday specifically focuses on the female perspective. A 'lost German girl' 'walks death's road' and surveys the destruction of World War II. A female voice ponders 'how different it would have been' if mythology and life had happier endings. Throughout this collection, Monday combines the past and present: movie directors and actresses of mid-20th century and 'the land of the electronic zombies' created by modern technology and social media. Each poem takes the reader on a nostalgic tour of the human experience."

— Abigail Schoolfield, Associate English Professor, Roane State Community College

"In *Bergman's Island and Other Poems*, history's wisdom and truth lie scattered across the modern age. The immensity of their brokenness is an ocean's weight that stuns with its 'disintegrated fish bones,' the ruins that humans seek to contain and make familiar 'like artificial snow in a glass winter globe.' These poems caution against replacing cultural mythologies with personal ones, for in doing so, we risk becoming islands that tremble and sink beneath the tides of what we cannot retrieve. Ralph Monday asks how we might learn from history if we regard it merely as an amusing curio and warns that we can love only if we understand the timeless commonality of suffering and doubt. In a cadence pairing the rhythms of human longing and resolve, this collection proposes that we find meaning in loss by fathoming the depths that surround each of us, by stirring 'the dark between the stars.'

— De'Anna Stephens, Associate Professor of English, Roane State Community College

For one of the greatest
brothers a man could ever
have. So many years &
so many memories from
the 1970's until now,
2021. Hope for many
more years of fellowship,
For Randy, my Brother.
Love you, man!
The Outing   July 30, 2021
Ralph Mendaz

ALSO BY RALPH MONDAY

All American Girl and Other Poems

Empty Houses and American Renditions

Narcissus the Sorcerer

Humanities: Journeys from the Paleolithic to Postmodernism, Vol. 1

Bergman's Island
AND OTHER POEMS

RALPH MONDAY

Sheridan, WY
Terror House Press
2021

EDITOR

Matt Forney (mattforney.com)

LAYOUT AND COVER DESIGN

Matt Lawrence (mattlawrence.net)

Excerpts of this book were published, in somewhat different form, by the following magazines and websites: *Crack the Spine, GFT Press, Ink, Sweat, and Tears, Subprimal Poetry,* and *Terror House Magazine.* The author would like to thank each publication for their support.

TERROR HOUSE PRESS, LLC

terrorhousepress.com

TABLE OF CONTENTS

INTRODUCTION

Why write poetry? Simply a rhetorical question, perhaps, but in this age of diminishing readership of any type of text, let alone the unique challenges of poetry, why create works that will most likely have a minimal readership? For me, the answer is simple: I believe that poetry is the highest form of art that no other aesthetic medium can approach; not film, music, painting, drama, or fiction. The uniqueness of poetry lies in the fact that none of the above mentioned can express the totality of the human condition, that only poetry says what cannot be said any other way: what it means to be human from something as ancient as the *Epic of Gilgamesh*, to the subjectivity of 19th century Romanticism, or something more recent as the High Modernism of *The Waste Land*. Good poems express the real, the subjective, the objective, the metaphysical nature of being, of ways of *knowing* that transcend the actual and express the mythical, archetypal nature of human existence. Poetry gets at being and meaning in manners challenging the reader both emotionally and intellectually through the use of figurative language, especially a well-wrought image like Pound's dictum: "An image is that which presents an intellectual and emotional complex in an instant of time." So of course, I am a Modernist. I disdain postmodern poetry for what the majority of it really is: poorly written narcissistic whinings of a self-indulgent, undisciplined generation that believes that history began at the moment of individual birth. For poetry to be great or even good, the poem must encapsulate the universal human condition. The poem must sing to all in every clime, time, and situation. The reader should come away with personal satisfaction, a new way of looking at the world, an epiphany of being. If that is the case, the poet has done his/her job, for writing poetry is a lonely endeavor, a plumbing of human consciousness in all its manifest subtleties.

Here then is an offering that I hope meets the reader's expectations. Here are presented images that, hopefully, will meet the demands of Pound, images that might engender a sudden sense of liberation, of freedom from time and space limits, of immediate and profound growth that brings us all closer to the realm of unknown, ontological being, so that we might touch the face of what cannot be said, but only imagined in words, the art of the hidden sublime.

There is only one poem in the collection that I will speak about, and that is the concluding work, "Sunday Morning a Century After: An Homage." November 2015 saw the 100th publication anniversary of Stevens' "Sunday Morning," one of the greatest poems of the 20th century. In homage, I wrote my version based on the original structure of "Sunday Morning." Like the original, my homage contains eight stanzas of fifteen lines each written in unrhymed blank verse. However, other than the structural organization, the poem is my original creation in that it has the woman in Stevens' poem, speaking now from the grave, pondering the questions raised in "Sunday Morning" from the vantage point of 100 years later. I certainly hope that the reader enjoys this poem and the entire collection. If so, my labor is fruitful.

Ralph Monday

LOST GERMAN GIRL

I see her in the YouTube video,
faded color, war's disillusionment
etched like veins of dark coal
beneath her eyes
                    her face.

She walks death's road in late spring
1945, like some exiled German Antigone,
bodies on either side, the black sweater
a robe a ferryman would wear on the
river of the
                    dead

covering her slender form as some
crematory shroud.

Face bruised by some laughing
god, or Russian soldiers after they
had their way with

her.

Still, her cheeks are chiseled fire
strokes, tangled mass of hair
burnt wheat field stubble.

She looks into the camera like
one staring at the underworld's
                gates,

before turning away
and the film whispers
                remember.

THE BONES OF MAY

Berlin, May 1945, what was once a
woman.
The ghost doesn't know she is a ghost,
no legs, torso, arms or hands, but a
fashion sense
still remains for the latest
lipstick, store shop dresses, high heels;
phantom taste buds
long for fresh tomatoes, cool drinks and
Moroccan coffee.

The rubble filled streets that she walks
without legs—this is a desert made by
cold machines releasing yards and yards
of bones.

Once a woman, a spirit now nothing to say.
Nothing to ponder.
Walk this broken concrete made coffin-stones
shaded by varying light, her Führer

3

a burned mausoleum stretched somewhere
in blue shade.

What is she now—unwarmed staleness, a
voiceless spell scratched on rough stone,
some broken doll from memory. For the
living a thought-form being whose atoms
still maintain substance, energy, blown about
in mad waves for priests to make senseless
incantations with crosses and cauldrons.

Condensed to primal essence, this she of
lost atoms, voice particles, song particles,
the moments of love and despair, young
kisses at night
no internet archive can reclaim this vanished pixel.

Not to go backward,
not to watch the soldiers,
the women, the children
reeled in sepia reverse by a
documentary film catching the
edge of the chapel door.

Not to go backward

the bones of May
passing all the forgetful
faces.

She sees herself in the film
walking, walking, foiled with
redness, thinking, thinking—*that
girl is not me. That girl is dead,* and
she will in her scattered atoms
forget everything by the end of this
shattered street.

Forget history
forget self
forget home
that hurts when turned
to a face lost in a
mangled alphabet

of noise, propaganda
of living and turned to
dig up joy from the soil
from the edge of dirty waters,

found only that the bones would
do, those bones of May
that dissolution of imagery
moving from one door
to another.

BERGMAN'S TRUTH

Panorama of the human condition
filmed by a machine's voracious eye &
splashed across silver screens—illusions for
a primed audience.

Bergman as magician emotionally manipulating a
people frame by shamanic frame. Come
into the confessional, the dark rows of popcorn &
drink filling the mouth as filmic rosaries.

Here is your salvation. Here is your silver cross.
Let me show you your truth, your lost
meanderings from month to month, the walking in
circles, paralyzed like a wheelchair bound

cripple by your own unconscious anxieties.
You do not understand that movies have become
your religion. Unknowing that art abandoned the
creative determination when separated from worship.

I have become the unwilling high priest who builds
now the cathedral in air for the masses without a
mass. There where you bleat your loneliness without
listening to others.

Drink the camera's wine, eat the lens as a
machined Eucharist, eternally walk in your
tired circles without knowing the true from the
false.

Behind you, at the theater's back, the dark rolls
through like a climax, like a dénouement, like
an army searching for Christ's spear after they
cast it into the still waters.

You move in a room of dreams, of twilight
scene after scene, searching for the music,
aching for the priest, for the confessional
instant that anoints the abandonment,

but you will never know for you embrace your
demons like a lover, like the gossip who never
inspects the source—your politics are peripheral,
checked at the door with the unread script.

SYNTAX OF NOTHING

Undesirable, though not untouchable the
weather wears her as a divine
spiral like autumn skirts tight about the
hemlines of waiting trees.

Her dancing is adored though he can no
longer join in, because she is gone into
the waves, her last story spit out, etched
on the tongue like some epileptic explanation,

muddy syntax vibrated out by someone
else explaining that the rain we once
walked through is razored now, and
though October fattens through round grapes,

acorns, no microphone can hold the red
scribbled song that you sang before
your last smile to me spread like a
bruise

on a potter's clay wheel, and
I could not catch a single note,
could not be angry at God,
could do nothing but listen to nothing.

THE MYTH UPON THE WHEEL

This is how I would know you—
perched on will's never ending
storm

buffeting laborious windmills
weaved by a spurned
imagination that you crave

where you walk in a night
that is the color of a woman's
legs.

The mind under the moon
becomes a river without
a ferryman

that shivers like a necklace
thrown about at a dance
for the sisterhood of the living dead.

Angering for life,
attuned to the motion
of sounds

you are placed upon the wheel
that will survive the myths
and read your life as fluent bronze,

as graven images and simulacrum
where thoughts are welded
to flesh and bone.

This is how I would know you—
a never satisfied mind
a woman dancing with long hair

to old songs filled with forgotten
words
of affluent poverty

burst into
flakes
of flames,

a partridge held as a fleeting moment
in the hand before flying
into a dead dawn.

UNREQUITED HARMONY

She gazed at the bookshelves behind her
therapist: Freud, but no Jung or Skinner.
The therapist, musing at her over his
cigar, as he had done for a decade,
thought that somewhere along the way
she had lost her original harmony.

He listened to her self-made myth,
an eternal war, a continually moving
day to day movie frame, she the star
actress.

Simulacrum conjured up like a bare
mannequin painted over with the day's
chosen colors, she said that she
heard from the past a
saxophone blowing out forgotten meaning.

The horn that he blew like some wingless
angel on a rooftop

shreds her thoughts like papier-mâché,
a piñata that cannot be burst even without
a mask.

A piece of flecked amber floats on her throat
as she herself hangs inside his vanished
tunes, plays the part again and again,

while her therapist watches through sullied
glasses, bored with the same non-reconciliation,
eternal act three frozen like the red ear-rings,
suspended statues, blood-drops arcing down
from her pierced flesh, the way that
he bloodied her with his music,

those lost tunes forever save in the
movie of the mind, and like the therapist's
thoughts, floats away.

DEER LODGE

They had known one another since crimson
youth; now the time was that of leaf-glued autumn
forest floors where they walked on the deck there
above Deer Lodge.

Friends since the time when her hair was pumpkin
pie braids, she had always been his female cartographer and
placed on her mental map that even young he had the black
lakes of an old man's eyes.

He reached out to touch her hand now, oil poured in
trembling sacrament, while the leaves tumbled in a cold
wind; she knew the violet bruises deep in the mind, knew
to trowel on love in quiet moments where gratitude redeems the
undone.

She took his hand and held it while memories patched
together like a pieced quilt their long ago imponderable, unspoken
insults, thoughts like streaking snow sleds, steeples brightened
by a young girl's laughter.

She remembered when they walked on the smoking,
burning water, her skirts like architraves, and he cried to her
about glasses of spilled love-juices, about the many bad poems
written about clichéd death.

She spoke: *people say to know beauty is inevitable loss,
inescapable grief, that this capacity separates us   from animals. I
am not sure   for I have seen grief flow   like water from animal
tongues.*

*To know death may be to know love—if so what kind of
love? Our shadow   follows us all our lives   disappears when
we do   does the shadow know heaven   does an Egyptian funerary
boat row it to the sun?*

*Does it matter? Claw marks precede us when we slide wet
from our mother's thighs, texted-tombstone our marker, all that is
left vapid images, lying reels in film cans. Is this the love we bring
into the world?*

*something black about it
something onyx
like a Slava Old-New Year
waiting for the
final diaspora.*

IN PRAISE OF SPOKEN DIFFERENCES

Books always do this to her
unfathomable books on bottomless
themes that she sits reading in a red
dress in the fall leaves, mind clothed
in scarlet thoughts.

Have you ever thought of this,
she asks me

to pull Moby Dick from the waters
a great white light swallowing transgressions,
crucified upon the sea, upon frothing waves—
crests tipped pink by his sacrificed blood?

How different it would have been
if her faith had survived.

How different would it have been on

the island if Ralph and Piggy had
never found the conch shell?

    Almost a thing of abstract art
her father died when she was seven,
splattering his brains all over the garage

    walls in wet grays and reds with a 12
gauge while she and her brother slept
upstairs.

    How different it would have been if he
hadn't lost his job, wasn't depressed,
if his girlfriend had stayed.

    How different would it have been if
Hamlet never toyed with Ophelia, if
Gertrude spurned Claudius?

    At forty her husband left her for a younger
woman, without remorse, without explanation,
gone like a shadow that ceased following its matter.

    How different would it have been if
Abelard kept his balls, Heloise never
donned the habit?

    How different would it have been if
Iseult had not told Tristan the sails

were black?

How different would it have been if
Romeo and Juliet changed the ending
of west side story?

Not such a small thing these
pantomimed silhouettes dancing like
Macbeth's witches

Not such a small thing.

Transgressions follow like
mosquito's multifaceted eyes,
locked in the vast deep the way
that only a special human can
hear humpback whales compose great
cetacean epics in celebration.

There in the deep quiet black where
disintegrated fish bones fall, float eerily down
like artificial snow in a glass winter globe.
Ocean snow covering the mud like watery
hoarfrost—these are the Saharas of the
abyss.

She swims
She swims
Deep

Deep

What would it be like if I had never been born?
What would it be?

How different would it have been to
never be?

How different would it have been?

MY TRIBE

I live in the past—a sense of urgency possesses
me like some eager ghost ardent to come alive
and taste again the language of the living.

Must be the wine of age that uncorks these
bygones, congenital disposition marking
totemic tales through a glass screen.

I am convinced that the 1940's, 50's was a
tribal time, at least that is my illusion lighting my
skin and making it glow.

But doesn't every generation look back at a better
world, the search for the lost home ingrained
within the soul?

Troubadours, all, at some still point, the
grass, the garden, the breathing earth singing,
singing out in symphonic arias.

Irony that I relive these times as digital days,
the postmodern computer an electronic time
machine

    transcending ticking moments, vanished
space. YouTube resurrects a wealth of American
myth—1950's high school proms

where tie and jacket youth, already men, smile
and escort young women wearing classy evening
dresses.

    Cheerleaders and ball games and school
bells ringing end of classes, real blackboards,
chalk—

American dream before the nightmares began.
Even the black and white trees lining small town
streets

    bow in the homage laden wind,
water hydrants patiently wait to spray out,
cool, hot summer days.

The smooth greasers and the cool beatniks are
no more than jesters, school jackets emblems of pride.
But all just digital now, ones and zeroes

    marking my silent brow.

Gone gone as mythical as Adam and Eve,

but a genesis sustaining nonetheless.

SELF-PILGRIMAGE

This was a pilgrimage of sorts, unconscious,
that she did not know, only felt like the river
turned to glass beneath the bridge,   beneath
the humming tires.

She crosses the asphalt toward the peculiar
momen   t   behind her the bowl of sky
splashed out as petroglyphs long forgotten,
like ancient sailors who   thought they would

fall off the end of the world. The light on her was a
despondent thing—when she slept her ex
haunted her as death sauntering   down the street
dressed in coat and tails.

The rusted metal roots hated by wind and rain
    press down upon her—pounding dead
memories   that she never wants to   resurrect,
yellowed bones fermenting in dirt.

In the North Carolina mountains a   Cherokee
    shaman gave her a red-tailed hawk's
feather from his hat   saying *you need vision.*
She dreamed different tales that   night—

diverse shadow women that came to her
    narratives floating from their   mouths
like bursting poppy seeds:
matter cannot be   transfigured into wine,

rattling bones tell the story, the rattler   always
    sleeping in rocks   cold frozen from the
winter. Have red hair   not blonde   stay
away from Roman statues   with broken off

noses—that's where the demon   lived.
    A man in the form of a swan or   bull
is not to be trusted. Fertility masks are
wasted if you belong to a tribe   ovulating

for nothing.
    Know that all is a   degenerate
floating parable   you   like us
walking within   covenant ground away.

THEY SING

They sing, you see, those
who embrace brothel's providence
whether with a whore in a backstreet
alley or within the shelter of heresy.

They would know heralds to
test their mettle with woman or god
or man—reason narrowed they see
in a chalice of uncertainty windows

sigh, optics decompressed by
desire. This is a nightmare of intellect,
no fruits bloom whether on tundra or
the haven of weeds.

With their songs they have made of
the earth a courtroom of disorder, truants
hunkered down wishing to change, to be
telepathic waifs.

The modern long discarded they would
deconstruct memory's attic, scrutinize the eighteenth
century nursery of suffering that brought them
here

where clouds sew and stitch together the
burial shroud, make of reason a lost graveyard,
preshrunk, centrifugal energy long spun out, not
even a cairn left to mark the spot.

Their songs burnish, meld, solidify that
which is believed to be an eyestrain—pirates of
their own past, intoxicated by desire to destroy
what was,

they mimeograph a tundra of oppression,
sweep away like weeds the last final traces of
a closeted majesty as leaves blasted by a newly created
dissonant eyrie.

THROUGH THIS GLASS

The coffin lowered into the wet earth
Like a seed sleeping through winter
The way of the father in life as in death
Dust to dust ashes to ashes

I never knew him, not really. 56 years
and we barely had a handful of   words,
maybe only when he was   sitting under a
tree,   whittling, sun on his   face.
   They will rest from their labor for
   their deeds will follow them

Walking away through the bare winter
trees, tombstones static stone texts   marking
the now nothing that was something, that is
nothing—his house empty   the bible the
black bible that he never comprehended
lying on a side table, mute, empty.
   The body that is sown is perishable;
   sown in dishonor, sown in weakness

His face framed behind glass in the hallway
eyes   Norse blue   of fjords   driven
by a weathered moon   that   had
tasted the steppes haunted moors
and they   followed me   like gently
praying eyelids   where darkness
liquefies   freezes over the masked
frost on glass   time of sleeping   of
unsaid evening prayers.
     Though you are evil, know how to
     give good gifts to your children

Alone alone I build the fire in the   woodstove
the way his bony black fingers from the
mine would set flame   mind-bonfires
licking like the blaze   from a burning
bush   as god speaking bible messages.
     who maketh his angels spirits;
     his ministers a flaming fire

Stripped of all reason   fall on the floor
saying words I do not know   I breathe life
into his still   image   where he comes
down off the wall and goes into the
late-winter naples yellow evening   behind
the thin pencil dark trees.
     Rise up and shine,
     for your light has come

where he comes from the glass   drives
on the wet dark roads through   hollers
the almighty father photograph   breathed
life   riding again through the long night
while wifechildren huddle   wait
for the nomad time of desert women in
thin silks hunted by the plucked
word from moonlight   moonlight
    But come here,
you sons of a sorceress

And he comes from the glass   breathes
in the scent of bars   of Appalachian
saloons   knows how the moon's gray
eye   the will of beasts   angels
sequined harlots takes one to the
mountains   to the stale   stolid
waters   running as blood   bitter
waters baptized by wine   where
the glass reflects this for a time   and
the solemn wind brings no song.

DIRTY MOONS

A beer joint in Kentucky deep in the mountains is no
city of mystery, maybe for a boy dragged in by his
drunken father to drink more and ogle the tight-
skirted whores.

I guess he thought the place was some seductive
burrow but you could smell the piss and the
blood, the landscapes of bigotry years-ground
into the angry floorboards.

The whores giggle and laugh and wait for some
body to finger them under their skirts if some
roughneck will buy them a drink or two—
laughing through ambition's cradle

dancers on a dark delta where the men with
their cold fingers dreamed they were stroking
cold virgins.

There is clear meaning:

love has stopped breathing. Hate is a dead skin
that cannot be sloughed off where only bleeding
kisses provide a sermon for transportation of all
the dead left coffin-eyed

on these numb floors   by
knife or gun or haunted wife who
would cauterize the memory and
rebirth through

emotion's pastiche—long married to
terrible sounds—this scene played
over and over, movie credits endlessly rolling
like

dirty moons.

CONSUMPTION

All her life she has been
eating herself.
As a girl beginning with her
feet where she washed the
feet of others with her long
hair.

Only at certain times was the
taste palatable.

At adolescence she consumed
her breasts before others could
take them.

Always she remained silent in the
agony. Though there was a little
blood, letting no one know, because
they could not understand,

except for the watcher following

when she slid from her mother's
loins,

always hushed but ever conscious
moving among shadows,
among dreams.

When she married she ate her
heart before it could be served
as a red roast to an unworthy
diner.

She ate her children, three
of them, one by one, a
child flesh-trinity lest

the world consume them as a
sacrifice to self.

At the end there was nothing
left to eat, not even

a thought.

THROUGH THESE SPACES

Each month drops of her
        blood
mirror the color of the Bradfords
in the backyard.

She would walk among the rain
        soaked
leaves as though moving to
catch a train to a space long lost.

Childhood teachers treated her as though
she was a
        puppet,
their bourgeois
manners reflected in long skirts that
trailed about the floor.

She made the pillows
        soft
for her

first husband,
           hard
as a cemetery
stone for her second,

for the tumults
of the years made her
           brittle,

her
apron replaced by
           nettled
thoughts.

She stopped looking at the
           photographs
of her dead children,

remembered only
her first love affair where they
           trekked

through frozen snow to the dirty
motel,

drank Mateus, listened to Sinatra
           singing
"My Way," had a kind of fumbling,
embarrassed sex.

They talked of meeting
again in the spring when the trees
              bloomed.
That was all it was—tongues making useless
chatter.

The trees never
              blossomed.
She would think of these things

at the morning mirror, knowing
that the space between the stars is
              dreadful,

cold. Comb out her long hair
              sing
all through the morning
light.

Sing as though calling the
sun to
              light

the trees full in the
disheveled
              spaces.

CHRISTMAS WITHOUT NORMAN

Last summer the young
evergreen got knocked
over by the lawn tractor.
Grew back toward the sun
in a great S curve.
A shame to cut it.
It grew so hard to live
But I did.
Tossed it on the fire
where I was burning
brush.

Erupted in a great
geyser of red flame
that even the rain
couldn't quench.
The cedar tree smelled like
Christmas.

Frankincense and myrrh
holly and cinnamon
so sweet
so nice
so Christmas
without Norman Rockwell

A DARK RENAISSANCE

A pooling of wet leaves remind me,
clumped there in summer's autumn
languor, despite all this late August
butterscotch light, that it is the dark,
the dark, that returns soon which never
left.

    No Renaissance maidens walk in the
sun. None remain.
If there were, they would say the shadows of the
leaves is dark enough for me.

    History is dark.
    Today is dark.

No matter how much one seeks the light,
drinks it in, let the summer sun bake
skin to a tanned sienna, dream of green
iguanas basking in the light—

the universe expands outward
flung by unknown dark particles.

Melodies of light never the dominant
tune, the vibrations of the sable cello
give song to those maidens walking in stubbled
fields where crows domino about and fiddle
the same earth theme on wet, beating wings.

History is dark.
Pages written in black ink.

The maidens themselves now part of concealed
stone, brunette song long faded, they
could not dip finger in night's inkwell, write
of the dark time like a court fool grinning at the
king.

They know the dark.
As before.
As now.

Long after the perishing expiration
date.

THE SENSE OF FEEL

Some feel the deep oceans. Some feel the
blackbird pecking at winter's crusted seeds.
Some feel cracking ice in spring thaw.
Others sense the universe expanding in the
bourbon dark, fragmented galaxies growing
further and further apart in the way of dead
relationships.

Feel or sense: a type of discernment, unconscious
recognition of nuance—the bird following
magnetic lines, the bear fat on fall's acorns, the
dusky wind carrying centuries' scents, the woman
in the window pulling on lingerie for the lover who
never comes.

Some feel the footsteps always walking—to
nowhere, to somewhere while some sense
the pregnant stroll will always be futile.

Even the leaves, the rocks, snow skimming

the ground, flowered trees, feel what can't
be felt, discarded lingerie the same.

Whether felt or sensed, the dark between
the stars grows ever larger, and earth
will not come walking forward to the
banqueting hall.

A PRAYER FOR THOSE WHO ARE PLUGGED IN

There is terror in the inarticulate,
those that do not read, have forgotten
history.

Those whose lives are controlled by
flickering images, momentary corporate
distractions living in the land of the
electronic zombies.

A prayer for those that are plugged in.

Images. Flick flick flick across screens in
homes, cars, mall and even meadow,

worship of the new god's tiny eye,
history in present pixels, 24 hour sound
bites where antiquity is Tiger, Beyoncé, Lady Gaga,
the lastest stuffed simulacrum, the ego-eye

honing in to feed, sounds and sights
carried in back pockets—

A prayer for those that are plugged in.

German crematoriums just another
image, Pol Pot some new rapper, crusades a
cool CD—they do not read, they twitter,
they do not see, they Facebook.

This terror has no time table, patiently
waits like blind albino termites building
mounds under the earth, chambers full and
fecund for all those that are plugged in.

SAME OLD SONG

Lately I've been wanting to return to the
seventies. We all want to return from
exile, somehow, someway, but Wolfe
was right, no way home again.

Trying hard though: listening in the
truck to "Crocodile Rock" and Carly Simon
singing "You're So Vain" while musing on all
the vain people that I have known.

This is like being put in a brown paper
sack for somebody else's lunch. I
want that feast, but you get too old
to eat, especially when you finally

realize that everybody is working
out of ego and fear. That drives them.
That along with biology and myth.
Everyone the center of his/her own

little myth—ego-lollipops rolled up
in the sex drive to be licked away
relationship through wasted relationship,
biology pulling them together like a

crocodile chewing on that week old
rotted gazelle corpse till they've had
their fill, woke up in yet another strange
bed wondering WTF—

till age catches up and biology no
longer matters. Gets to the point
that nothing matters. I sit at my
windowsill every morning drinking

coffee and thinking about this
while the sun comes up and the
birds wake up the day: little
narcissistic shits.

WAITING

You aren't waiting for Godot,
maybe you don't know what it
is. The waiting will end in some moment,
some probably commonplace experience, like
waiting for the mortgage payment to
post, or waiting for the microwave to
　　　　beep that the quiche is done.

The life is ordinary, American consumer in
middle age far removed from ISIS, Nazi Germany, feasting on
photoshopped images of physical perfection, just
waiting on that middle age spread, retirement,
　　　　Social Security and a 401k.

You have no recollection of the horrors of
Achilles, the terrors of blind Tiresias, the
incestuous madness of Oedipus, for your sense of
history is the latest sports column, who will win
the Super Bowl, World Series, who will go on a
major golf run—will it be Tiger or some new

kid on the block?

Waiting, like the dinosaurs waited for that immense
mountain to come hurtling in and force a cease to
all foraging, or the black death of the calamitous
13th century, all somehow akin to a dentist's visit,
a blockbuster movie of car chases, big, bad explosions,
a shoot-the-hell-out-of-the-bad-guy finale and "hero"
            take the feisty female.

Waiting for the negative news, stock market dip,
the latest CD by the latest, hottest new voice murmuring
nothing. So used to waiting and growing toward nothing
that even the girls in their thin summer dresses deserve
            hardly a glance.

Waiting.
Waiting.
    You are waiting for you.

WHAT GOOD IS LOVE?

I bet a lot of people have asked themselves
that question: Abelard after they took his
balls, Paris lying mortally wounded, Medea
spurned by Jason—but it's not just the mythic
amours, or television and movie trysts.

Common guys and gals have wrestled, like
Job's angel, with this question, all scratching
their heads in hormonal angst.

I mean, what good is it?
In this day and age love is sold as a
commodity, a panacea—strutted down
runways, soaked up at bars.

Portrayed as a magic cure all, the healthy
and the ill, the aged and the young, the
deranged and the semi-sane pursue this
Alice rabbit hoping not to get stuck in
some endless hole.

Really, what can you do with love?
It can't be measured, quantification is a
mathematician's nightmare, the banker can't
deposit it in your account and say this is the
value.

No measurable price like any other relative
thing: diamond, gold watch, a new car or
house. No, because what really blows people's
minds is the myth, the eternal Jason-quest
after the golden apples—some narrative
mystery that holds the secret to itself,
smiling, the underground hibernating seed—
waiting to hatch.

TO LISTEN

Listen, I told her. You are young, without
molding, little more than a new moon.
We sat upon a glacial carved rock, watched
the river's eyemusic far below the East Rim
run like a chorus from applause.

Someday, in the deep night between
covers, when he whispers of Isolde, pretend not
to hear.

When he tells you of the Lady with a bloody
knife sing to him, "Bringing to mind all the things I did,
So many that I can't recount them all in this tale: Going
in winter to waulkings and weddings…What remains of
Andrew's house, now full of nettles, Brings to mind when
I was young."[1]

Seduced by cities and media he will not know your
song, but sing anyway, sing till the stars walk the moon's

---

1   Mary MacPherson. "Longing for Home." 19th century Scottish ballad.

ladder down the sky.

We had come to this place of rock and mist, tree and wild to be within salvation's myth, to touch the core of a lightning nourished oak, be not drooped or feebled.

In those birth covers when he wants to
Eros the tale between your bereaved thighs, laugh of
Troy and Briseis buried in Agamemnon's armpits—call
yourself Mary the Magdalene who washes the sky with
her hair.

ALL THOSE YEARS

If I come to your window through the
littered leaves, if you sit at the mirror
in a nightgown brushing your scarlet
hair, will you remember all those years
when you read to me, the tongue of
books walking through all the world,
and you held my hand while the rain fell?

If I come to your window while you gaze
at old family photo albums as gray as moss,
as vibrant as vibrating photons, do you see
me there on a back page, looking...looking at
you?

If I come to your window while you dine on
Mediterranean oysters, soft pink mollusks
sautéed in white wine, butter, will you tip your nails
in my blood and circle the world in crimson?

If I come to your window and toss pebbles at the

glass, will you see me in the purple twilight clothed in
velvet knowing, remember decades past when you
fed me asparagus with green fingers and I
licked the thin sweat from your eyelids; afterwards
we slept on satin sheets and woke smiling?

If I come to your window will you wave and smile and
show me your red dress for the theatre and say
I love you one more time?

If I come to your window before you wore my
ring, if I can wheel myself there, return to a
time when we were, before the decades passed
and you left me not of your own free will, but
from the final call out there somewhere in
hibernating November fields, can you return?

if I come to your window.
if I come to your window.

TELL ME YOUR THOUGHTS

If I really knew you,

not just a virtual knowing,

not the geography of virtual

space, of mouse clicks, twitter,

emails that lack the romance of

old fashioned letters, the

ones that come in sturdy envelopes

carrying friendly vignettes, sincere

greetings, quaint antebellum times

gone out of fashion, I would sit at a

table with you outside the Roman Coliseum, as

friends, carry on a conversation over

wine as red as Homer said, "the wine

dark sea," goat cheese.

As a friend in comfortable surroundings,

I would ask, "tell me what you think of the

horrors of men in ancient battle here for the

pleasure of the crowd. Share with me your

ideas about your music, your poetry, the

wild heroines that people your novels.
Speak to me of your muse and whether
she comes in dreams, or as a creative
contemplation in a white gown bearing garlands of
flowers, or in a dark time, dark portents.
Tell me your thoughts on the planet,
all the people, shades now, who
have walked before, and those yet to
see frost or ice or smell fall's burning
leaves.

Tell me how you have lived, your successes,
failures, tell me your dreams, your
nightmares, the times that you have
laughed, the moments that you cried.

Tell me how music has choreographed
your life, how poetry has sustained you in
times of need.

Tell me all that you wish to tell, and those things
that you do not, for I will nod to you, clink
glasses, say, I know," while the sun
falls shadowed and silent on that great
hulking mass before us.

STILL LIFE WITH RANDOM THOUGHTS

Why can't we go back? Why must it always be
forward, like blind dust motes, like railroad
tracks that end at the docks?
There are silver finned fish there
laid out in the sun waiting for salt, for
brine, for a kiss that never comes.
The things that be, all the should nots,
like the girl in first grade that you loved,
where you wrote your names on the
desk, but she never loved you back. You
went into the cloakroom and cried, there
among the cedar smells, the mothballs
like tiny white moons, the dark cloths
that you burrowed into ashamed.

Later, outside the soda shop Billy Thomas
took your ice cream cone bought with your
last quarter. You knew there was no one to

wait on you, not now, not up the line. Not
ever. So you construct a still life based on
random thoughts where you walk like an
unseen Goliath into the mind painting and
squeeze out colored pigments that mark
what you would like to believe really
happened, but like a bleeding canvas
you are covered over in a crusted impasto, a
Munch scream not enough to erase the
cloakroom, the smell of yellow piss, the
eyes that never stop following.

TO ENDURE

Winter and snowing when he came upon
her. Gray shroud of Turin clouds hugging the
mountain tops, the wind blowing like it was
waiting for a clock to stop.

This was the Big South Fork at the East Rim
overlook. She had climbed over the chain link
barrier and stood on the cliff edge staring at a
thousand feet of air between her and the bottom.

Fall sassafras leaves red hair, the kind born to be
wedded to the earth, and staring, staring at the
river's rush and roar so far away.
It's not that bad, he said. *I've been there.*

Two things drive us, she replied. *Like that river
rushing to nowhere only to return to the source. Two
things. Biology and myth. Myth and biology. To fuck
and fight, make meaning of it all.*

To become a female Icarus with polyester wings, soar
between here and the moon, to fly with falcon vision
and seed the sky, a Venus of Willendorf stripped of
will breathing out the earth.

Fog extinguishes the hills, the river, she said. *The
fish fuck and fight and make good corpses for others
to do the same. I do not know you, but I do for all we can
know is the unknowing.*

To know the answer to Hamlet's question, the riddle of
Ophelia's love. To kiss the paws of the sphinx and hold
dinner conversation with an Egyptian mummy, there might the
puzzle be known.

*One small step, like Armstrong's, and I too, would be the flying
eagle visiting realms unknown. Strip off the wooden growth
rings, sprout grass from my mouth and lie down in a field
of stone.*

MAKING LOVE TO JAYNE MANSFIELD

I think of Jayne Mansfield, look at her
from various pictures gathered on the
internet: the brief black top and see-through
nylon pants, the sequined body dress barely
covering her vintage assets—in black and
white, color—she blooms
like a flash-flooded desert
chained by her own beauty.

Outlasting Warhol's nature of fame, still
a piteous framed creature flowing across
any cheap screen, now relegated to movie
myth,

impossible for the average woman to self-
identify, thing of romantic sublime gorgeousness,
what must her life have been like,

so dead now,
so alive.

THE FIRST OF SEPTEMBER

My mother's reflective stories, her memory of
what she believed my father to think that day in
1939 when he said the war would be over by
Christmas. The days of hunkering by the radio,
entire families listening to CBS live broadcast
Poland's invasion. The red and black swastika
not yet branded by airwaves on American foreheads,
my father's interests lay to the mountain top,
where the Murray twins swam in a frog-scummed
strip pond full of cattails and flagellating tadpoles
from mating season.

He thought of their shadowed crotches moving in
the September light, my mother said, of their young
breasts soon to be tipped by autumn's first frost.
He didn't drive to war; he drove a heaving and
gasping rusted pickup to watch them swim, gave them
rides home after bottles of beer and naked bodies
pressed into the grass.

Who knows Mother's mythologies of the mind that
she found from the vantage point of old age. The
quilted heat of that long ago day where love and war
fused in the mind like pieces of steel arced together
by a blowtorch.

He would leave her for a time, all the way past 1945
when the war's march ceased, his boots carrying
him through morning fog, dripping trees like alabaster,
the poised shotgun a marker in time, of moments past
and canned reels yet to project. Sometimes squirrels
fell from the blast that made stew for hungry children's
mouths.

When weary of dying in another woman's bed, he would
return, never knowing the story of Isolde or Tristan,
Paris or Helen, Heloise and Abelard. He had none of their
tragic honor, where the only black catastrophes he knew
were those of coal-dusted men returned from the underworld
each evening, to go to the creek in the woods, drink and
gamble.

She told me that when he lay dying in his bed pointing
to air and saying there is Betty Jane, you need to talk to
her, his mind ravaged by time and circumstance, German
boots long perished ghosts, that she forgave him, for what
he saw was vision, not flesh, an American moment, where
his myth met hers that would never be written in epic meters.

THE PAINTED SELF

Have you ever stared at a painting,
unconsciously realizing that to walk through
art is to see a self-reflection of particular
times? Looking for some way to know
self without knowing? Or maybe it is a
desire to live another life in another time.
Begin at the end with Van Gogh's *Wheatfield
with Crows.* That one is a rubber lined room
for any loss, the dog that no one loved, the
final fitful snores of a grandfather, the chatter
of machine gun fire near the end in Berlin, the
rejected whore's love.
Maybe a Picasso, *Girl Before a Mirror,* perhaps
fragmented reflections reflecting the fragments to
come.
Too harsh? Choose something light and breezy
like an impressionist landscape that makes you
want to wear a white dress and run barelegged
through a field of flowers.
Or a longing for home, Norman Rockwell and

golden browned turkeys, a smiling mother, a
pipe smoking sweatered father, children who
never grow old, doors never locked.
But enough of this, some greater distraction is
needed—a romp through a German cabaret,
dark and smoky, steins of Austrian beer,
willing women before the guns began.
And you, pinned to the pages of a book
waiting for something to put hooks in and
tell you that it's all ok.

RILKE'S ROOM

She said that Rilke wrote of a moment when
recognition blooms that individual death lies
waiting somewhere within the body.

Is it scripted, directed, by some unknown force living
beyond the stars?

But you must understand, she said, that is only one
kind of death. There are many others whose
cruelty afflicts the living.

A man and a woman as above so below, skies
mirroring mood whether sleeping or awake,
classical elements that philosophers said could
change us, make of through time

four winds at the four corners of the earth
living the death that we would become living
again

whether tree and rock become the mother
and father's voice, or our own, a wish of
the earth that makes us sharpen knives in
moments of insomnia,

to watch swarms of new wasps as
reminders of bruised waves unbalanced.

This is why the woman wears attractive
dress, red lipstick smeared across a
bloody past, the man to think only of
swords and an unknown rapture,

to stare at strangers just beyond periphery's
vision lost in songs of their youth,

and

know that the grave-grass, the gray
ghosts of burnt out desire
is what moves our moods as moon phases
crescent and full
emit no light but reflect
light released by another, and

in those moments of attempting to
walk a bridge between worlds of reconciliation
realize it is better to live with warm beasts

in their circled dance,
soft eyes mirroring bloodied forgiveness
that does not last.

TWO GIRLS

The girl lounged beside me
is not you, no Lucy to my
Charlie Brown. Not even the
surrogate I have stitched together for
decades like stretch marks elongated
over an eternal pregnancy.

You may as well be dead but still
wound round like an engine's copper coil.
I cannot jolt you out of the carpet,
your name still tangled in every thread.

Somewhere atoms seep still from your
molecules, the way that electricity streamed
from you like cream, and those wavelengths,
purple truths, illuminates a language that I cannot
speak.

Somewhere, worn down by earth's fingers, sky's
ardor, you must still intuit a strange version of the person

you thought you knew, the way that I look for a
shop still selling records, or a lost
child yearns for a way home.

You do not know the way I am now, nor I
you. If I could speak to you I would ask,
what is your night? Do you know the deep
dusk there where you kneel on smooth stones
expecting absolution?

I expect that you might say,
in those strange god-tongues—I have been this way
before, will be again, for it is rain-heavy bushes,
the moon like a broken light bulb that is fractured,
that cannot bite off a star.

And you, you must know that this is a false-
borne day, a dishonest December moment that
can only beguile.

THOSE DAYS ARE WHAT WE ARE

I live in the past now, most of my
life drawn out behind me like a
tightened string between two Campbell's
soup cans, the voices winging back and
forth between two boys whose vibrating
voices are ghost whispers fading into white
sound.

It is so much safer there, back in the 1940's,
50's. People are polite, women are ladies. I
can live a Norman Rockwell existence, eat
turkey at Thanksgiving with a whole family,
open Christmas presents and slide down a snowy
hill.

Everyone is alive—all my dead family and
friends, smiling, waving just like they do in the
photo albums—no need to worry about a heavenly
resurrection, or silent Eve's foraging among the
trees.

I can ride the bombers with pinup girls
and take out Hitler's madness, be the hero that
I never was.

I can go to the drive-in and watch Henry Fonda in a
black and white world protect the boy from the
mob in *Twelve Angry Men.*

I can eat real popcorn with real butter, have a Baby
Ruth that is as round as the end of a Louisville
slugger.

Drive a candy red convertible 56 T-bird out to
lover's lane and pin my high school sweetheart,
the love of my life that I lost long ago.

When I am done dream weaving, caught in my
own spider's lair, I can drive home to the house I
never had, listening to the Teen Queens singing
"Eddie My Love."

HOLY THEOTOKOS SAVE US

In the cathedral empty of true feeling,

the icons are beautifully silent: blue and
green hues, golden halos, the choir in
perfect harmonies taking us across time,
space, to the beginning days when the
naming began, where we began that which
brought us here—

Why is it that we cannot remake
childhood myths into adult
acceptance?

Why are we broken and torn by stories
of the damned?

The Trinity intoned and like rote childhood
conditioning, I murmur most Holy Theotokos
save us—

from our own evil we are taught,

from the two that ate the forbidden,
the ban passed down from birth to death
like stars that never cease shining

so we are broken on the rack
signs everywhere: in malls or
bedrooms or social media or all
the flickering images passed by like
kaleidoscope snapshots which define
the words sung out in church hymnals

of that mythic time when we were never
given a chance—

but perhaps salvation is

loving those outcast, like us,
pardoning the unforgiveable,
accepting all that is broken by
broken words,

knowing that we are really plucked

as a wet body from
wet earth,

that if the words are cast off
they cease to matter.

SUNDAY MORNING A CENTURY AFTER: AN HOMAGE

I.

Not so complacent in her dressing gown,

the sensuous world remains mused upon,

thoughts common to many still not dispersed

by sun, moon, heavens above, trinity

eternally present, each spring revived

in cathedral dreams. For a moment the

ancient calamity stilled by wide water,

until the quiet dead in muted voices

pass as a transparent procession in

a forgotten carnival parade. Then

no modern science can stem Jerusalem's

return to this day, crossing of water,

where dreams speak now of a quickened kingdom

inhabiting not only the mind, but

a crown of blood, a cross, a tomb, of mind.

II.

Is it conditioned conscience that makes you

reward the dead? Is the divine a thought

made manifest by the dreams of others?

Can you not find in fields, fruited trees, the

burning sun, fit things for worship? The self,

a century's disciplined lens for thought,

made material gauzy spirit quick

in divinity within. To exalt,
those eternal seasons must be tempered
in recognition of all autumn souls
who have felt the presence in stirring suns,
sap returning to the bough, a measure
of human joy and sorrow, summer's heat,
winter's crusted beard. Reality is
formed of mind—nature is the soul of thought.

III.

In mind's myth any number of gods was
theogony formed, motherless, the land
itself ancestor, eternal queen where
gods enthroned, sat with attendants musing
intermingled blood, human and divine.
Not even science, a world spanning web,
a tomb and cross, can banish the return.
Longing for heaven dissipated as
the Italian, the Pole, Gaia from dark
moon, beamed lack of virginal connection
for the spinning orb passed eternally
through heaven's gates. The sky a conduit
joined to earth by pencil flame, seat of gods
labor of return, love found in wet leaves—
paradise translated by mother's tongue.

IV.

"When the green cockatoo is gone," she says,
"contentment flies astray. Why do they not
return from dark autumn's embrace? Have they
no knowledge of paradise eternal?"

Century's two wars destroyed paradise
when mind could no longer comprehend that
savage desert dervish feasting on a
sacrifice. Apple's birth polluted by
an aged, impotent god, the land barren,
not even all the church choirs, seraphim,
could undo the wreck, that and two thousand's end,
Darwin's dance, physics' deep peer into the
heart of darkness, epiphany of matter—
May follows winter, endures as swallows
preening on green branches awaiting song.
V.
She says, "For serenities' sake my mind
must know whence I am gone what follows."
Obliteration is now key. The time
long past when gods walked among us like a
welcoming balm. Zeus, Mithras, heaven's hill
banished by thought's realm. Embrace now lover's
caress, autumn's leaves, sighs on wet thick nights,
for this too shall pass, all left but a memory
of those remaining behind as Achilles
sought Timê and kudos as an ointment
for memory lost in the above world.
These passions drive the sphere to bloom, maiden
to dream of eternal love's embrace; they
are unthought faith, desires in far setting
suns where girls sense their recurring equinox.
VI.
Is the eternal a static haven?

Do tender leaves never know autumn's red?
How can that which remains forever green
excite the lover when new seasons are
needed? Rivers run to the sea yet they
return whence they came. The sun forever
knows its dumb circuit in horizon's sweep.
The heart of paradise is seeker's thoughts,
not naked Eve before the tiger turned
away. Those that voice heaven's choir deprave
this moment's eternity. Asleep, or
shook by waking dream, October's slanted
light gives witness for dark sorrows returned
after winter's barren crust. There in sprouts
on forest floor the knowing awaits all.
VII.
The old god speaks its charms in rings of light
with naked men, bare women, equal as
their swanlike dance blends through tattooed drum beat.
A shapeless white moon, burgundy evening
sun, ungendered conductors, symphonic
nature's metronomy keeping time as
in the first eyelids of morning, these twinned
dancers measure the earth's turning tune as
a cathedral beneath bare feet. This is
the fire burning in heaven, angelic,
that makes of rock a pew, of leaves, choir book.
Let this be thought's funeral—where men and
women drink river's communion cup, the
dawn's blessing brings sacrament's earliest

kiss where they go and come from liquid fog.
zShe returns to silent waters, whether
in dream or Darwin's reality, a
procession of ghosts walk backwards through time's
gates, all that have ever been. She is but
a flicker among them, shade not quickened
by Calvary's hushed call. The wilderness
of bird choirs, flowers and orchards shall be
all final rites watched over by heaven's
hanging lights—this is enough, the savage
old mother a soothing maiden and crone.
She would hear their disembodied, still tongues,
fly with them to know if Orphean songs
quicken their step. They, like the morning dew
proceding darkness, do not pause—fellowship
ambiguous, baptized by still, black waters.

ACKNOWLEDGMENTS

Many thanks are offered to the following journals and editors where some of these poems originally appeared. Without the selfless and untiring toil of the individuals who work long hours to bring poetry to an audience, the words in the following pages may have lain mute and unread.

"Bergman's Island," "Bergman's Truth," "Consumption," "Syntax of Nothing," "Unrequited Harmony," and "Two Girls": *Terror House Magazine*.

"Holy Theotokos Save Us" and "The Sense of Feel": *Ink, Sweat, and Tears*.

"In Praise of Spoken Differences": *Subprimal Poetry*.

"Silent Screens": *GFT Press*.

"Sunday Morning a Century After: An Homage": *Crack the Spine*.

ABOUT THE AUTHOR

Ralph Monday is Professor of English at Roane State Community College in Harriman, Tennessee and has published hundreds of poems in over 100 journals. His books include *All American Girl and Other Poems* (2014), *Empty Houses and American Renditions* (2015), *Narcissus the Sorcerer* (2015), and a humanities text published by Kendall/Hunt in 2018. Volume 2 of the humanities text is expected in 2021.

terrorhousepress.com

CPSIA information can be obtained
at www.ICGtesting.com
Printed in the USA
LVHW111323020421
683314LV00019B/148